EARTH'S CHANGING
WEATHER
and CLIMATE ™

Droughts
of the Past and the Future

Karen Donnelly

The Rosen Publishing Group's
PowerKids Press™
New York

To my family: Cathy, Colleen, and David

Published in 2003 by The Rosen Publishing Group, Inc.
29 East 21st Street, New York, NY 10010

First Edition

Editor: Gillian C. Brown
Book Design: Michael J. Caroleo

Photo Credits: Cover, title page, page borders, pp. 15, 16 © Weatherstock/Warren Faidley; back cover, pp. 8, 12, 20 © Digital Vision;   p. 4 (center) © Nova Development Corporation; pp. 4, 11 © Artville; p. 7 © CORBIS;
  p. 19 © Eyewire.

Donnelly, Karen
Droughts of the past and the future / Karen Donnelly.— 1st ed.
  p. cm. — (Earth's changing weather and climate)
Includes bibliographical references and index.
Summary: Discusses the importance of water on earth, what a drought is, conditions that can cause droughts, and the possibility of droughts in the future.
  ISBN 0-8239-6217-2 (library binding)
1. Droughts—Juvenile literature. [1. Droughts.] I. Title.
  QC929.25 .D66 2003
  551.57'73—dc21
                                                                    2001006660

Manufactured in the United States of America

Contents

Water's Many Uses

Every day each person in the United States uses thousands of gallons (l) of water. Many of us do not realize how much water we use or from where it comes. When we have a hamburger for lunch, we do not think about the water that was needed to grow wheat to make flour for the bun. We do not think about the water used to grow hay and corn to feed the cattle used for the burger meat. If we add french fries and a soda to our hamburger, about 1,500 gallons (5,678 l) of water was used to make the entire meal.

Water is our most important natural resource. Without water everything on Earth would die. When there is not enough rain and snow for a long time, the land becomes cracked and dry. We have a drought.

Water has no color, smell, or taste in its pure form.

What Is a Drought?

A drought is when there is lower than average **precipitation** over an extended period of time, sometimes for as long as several years. Precipitation brings water from the **atmosphere** to the land. Rain, snow, sleet, and hail are types of precipitation. Droughts occur when the normal amount of precipitation and **evaporation** is upset. Evaporation is when water changes into a gas and returns to the atmosphere. When a puddle dries up, it is because of evaporation. This repeated movement of water from the atmosphere to the land and back into the atmosphere is called the water cycle. To understand droughts, it is important to understand the water cycle.

It is normal for little rain to fall in the desert. In some deserts, the rainfall is less than 1 inch (2.5 cm) of precipitation a year.

The Water Cycle

The water cycle moves water from Earth to Earth's atmosphere and back again. Water is made up of tiny units called **molecules**. When water in oceans, lakes, and rivers absorbs heat, the molecules begin to move apart. They evaporate and change to a gas called **water vapor**. When you wash your hands and don't dry them with a towel, the water evaporates. This is the water cycle in action.

In the United States, the atmosphere holds 40 trillion gallons (151 trillion l) of water! On the same day, 4 trillion gallons (15 trillion l) of this water falls to Earth as precipitation. Some of the water soaks into the ground or runs into rivers and streams, but more than half of it evaporates. When there is not enough precipitation, a drought can happen.

A birch tree gives off 70 gallons (264 l) of water daily. This evaporation of water from plants is called transpiration.

Precipitation

Water vapor rises into the atmosphere where the air is colder. As it rises, the water molecules cool, move closer together, and turn back into tiny droplets of liquid water. This is called condensation. The droplets bump against each other and stick to form larger and larger drops. When they are too heavy to stay in the atmosphere, they fall to the ground. The water that falls back to Earth is precipitation and is an important part of the water cycle.

Droughts happen when the water cycle gets interrupted and precipitation decreases. There are several ways in which the water cycle can be interrupted or changed, such as higher temperatures on Earth and changes in weather patterns.

In warm air, water droplets will be rain. In cold air, water droplets will freeze and fall as sleet, snow, or hail.

Global Warming

The average global temperature has increased about 1°F (.5°C) over the past 100 years. However, over the last 10,000 years the temperature increased one degree every 1,000 years!

People seem to play a large part in the planet's warming. Since the **Industrial Revolution**, we have burned larger amounts of fossil fuels, like gas, coal, and oil, to heat our homes and power our cars. This increased use of fossil fuels sends **carbon dioxide** into the air. Since the Industrial Revolution, the level of carbon dioxide in the air has increased 30 percent. Some scientists are concerned that the increase in Earth's average temperature, called global warming, may cause more droughts.

Nine hundred million tons (816 hundred million t) of coal are used in the United States each year.

The Greenhouse Effect

There are many gases that make up Earth's atmosphere. Carbon dioxide, along with other greenhouse gases in the atmosphere, helps keep the Earth warm through the greenhouse effect. Like the glass walls of a greenhouse, carbon dioxide traps heat from the Sun. This makes Earth's surface warm enough for life.

Scientists believe that one cause of drought is warmer temperatures on Earth. Higher temperatures cause faster evaporation and can also change weather patterns. When more water evaporates there is less water on Earth's surface. A change in weather patterns can mean less precipitation than usual. Both of these changes could cause drought.

Without the greenhouse effect, the Earth would be about 50°F (27°C) cooler.

Drought and La Niña

The wind moves moisture in the atmosphere around the globe. When the normal air currents are interrupted by abnormal weather patterns, such as La Niña, drought can result.

During La Niña, the **polar** jet stream moves south and pushes cold, northern air down from its normal pattern across Canada and the northern United States. When La Niña happens, **subtropical** winds, which usually bring moisture from the south, are weakened. Less rain falls in the southwestern United States during La Niña. This creates a drought. A drought in the southwestern United States, where conditions are already very dry, affects farmers' crops and can be very costly. La Niña usually follows a period of **El Niño**, another unusual weather pattern.

During droughts in western Texas, people try to use less water.

Drought and Fire

During a drought, soil dries and cracks. Plants **shrivel** up. Dry, brittle leaves carpet the ground. In 1988, the worst drought in 50 years affected 35 states. Rainfall totals in the northern Midwest and the Rocky Mountains were from 50 to 85 percent below normal. Forest fires raged, and 600,000 acres (242,811 ha) of Yellowstone National Park burned in Montana, Wyoming, and Idaho.

Scientists are concerned about another effect that fires have on the environment. Smoke from fires sends huge amounts of carbon dioxide and methane, another greenhouse gas, into the atmosphere. Some scientists worry that when many fires burn in a year, the increase in greenhouse gases may contribute to global warming.

Fires do not permanently damage a forest because fire is a natural part of a forest's life cycle. Here a forest regrows after a forest fire.

Drought and Deserts

Deserts expand during a time of drought. In Africa, the Sahara, the world's largest desert, has begun to expand. This process is called **desertification**. Desertification is almost impossible to stop once it begins.

The Sahel is a vast grassland area that lies at the southern border of the Sahara. During a dry year, the grasses along this border dry up and the sands of the Sahara move in. If no rain falls the next year, more grass will die. Beginning in 1968, the Sahel experienced a drought that lasted for five years. As the grasses of the Sahel **withered** and died, the desert spread southward. When the balance between rainfall and evaporation is upset by drought, **drylands** that had sustained life can become **barren.**

More than 2 billion people live in drylands. That is nearly 40 percent of the world's population.

Droughts of the Future

The dust bowl drought happened in the Great Plains of the United States during the 1930s. It was severe and widespread. This drought caused millions of people to move to the western United States to look for jobs.

Some scientists are concerned that global warming may lead to more frequent and longer periods of drought. They think that future droughts will be worse than the dust bowl.

However, not all scientists agree that global temperatures will continue to rise. What we know for certain is that global populations continue to rise. More and more people will need water. Drought, which leads to disease and starvation, looms as one of the most serious and dangerous results of global warming.

Glossary

atmosphere (AT-muh-sfeer) The layers of air surrounding the Earth.

barren (BAR-in) Unable to produce plants.

carbon dioxide (KAR-bin dy-OK-syd) A gas that plants take in from the air and use to make food.

desertification (dih-zer-tih-fuh-KAY-shun) A change in landscape from a grassland to a desert, sometimes caused by drought.

drylands (DRY-landz) An area with more rain than the desert but not enough to support agriculture.

El Niño (EHL NEEN-yo) A warming of ocean water in the tropical Eastern Pacific Ocean When El Niño becomes strong, it can affect weather worldwide.

evaporation (ih-vah-puh-RAY-shun) Changing from a liquid to a gas.

Industrial Revolution (in-DUS-tree-al reh-vuh-LOO-shun) Changes in the way factories and farms worked that began in England in the late 1700's. Many new machines, like the steam engine, that need fossil fuels to run, were invented.

molecules (MAH-lih-kyoolz) Tiny building blocks that make up a substance.

polar (POH-lar) Having to do with the North Pole or the South Pole.

precipitation (prih-sih-pih-TAY-shun) Any form of moisture that falls from the sky.

shrivel (SHRIH-vul) To dry up and shrink.

subtropical (sub-TRAH-pih-kul) Regions that are right next to tropical regions.

water vapor (WAH-ter VAY-pur) water in the form of a gas.

withered (WIH-therd) To have shrunk.

Index

Web Sites

To learn more about droughts, check out these Web sites:

www.noaa.gov

www.enso.unl.edu/ndmc